D0849486

Prince Charles, growing up in Buckingha
J 941.085 GIL   221279

Gilleo, Alma,

MAY 27 '82   DATE DUE
DEC 16 85

J   1723
941.085
GILLEO, ALMA
Prince Charles Growing Up

OVERSIZE

LONGLAC PUBLIC LIBRARY

PRINCE CHARLES
Growing Up in Buckingham Palace

by Alma Gilleo
illustrated by Helen Endres

THE CHILD'S WORLD

ELGIN, ILLINOIS 60120

Library of Congress Cataloging in Publication Data

Gilleo, Alma.
  Prince Charles, growing up in Buckingham Palace.

  SUMMARY: Briefly describes the childhood of the heir
to the British crown.
  1. Charles, Prince of Wales, 1948-   —Juvenile
literature. 2. Great Britain—Princes and princesses—
Biography—Juvenile literature. 3. Great Britain—
History—Elizabeth II, 1952-   —Juvenile literature.
4. Buckingham Palace—Juvenile literature.
[1. Charles, Prince of Wales, 1948-   2. Princes]
I. Endres, Helen. II. Title.
DA591.A33G54   941.085′092′4 [B] [92]   78-18938
ISBN 0-89565-029-0

Distributed by Childrens Press, 1224 West Van Buren Street, Chicago,
Illinois 60607.

© 1978 The Child's World, Inc.

All rights reserved. Printed in U.S.A.

Outside Buckingham Palace, a crowd of people waited for some special news. It was a cloudy day in November. As night came, more people joined the crowd.

Then a door opened, and one of the Queen's pages ran toward the crowd.

"It's a boy!" he said. The people cheered. Princess Elizabeth had a son.

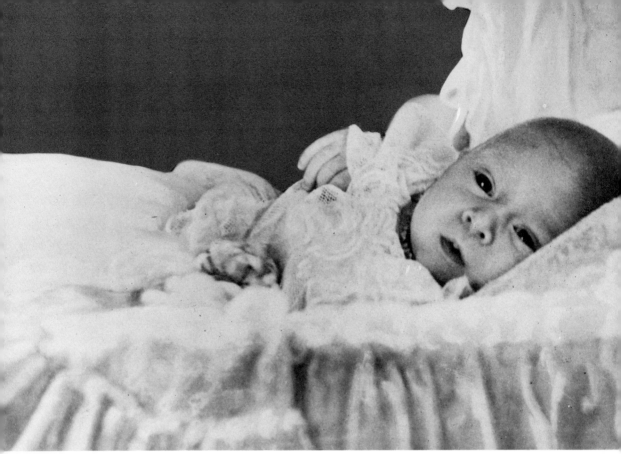

Prince Charles, one month old.

The baby prince was named Charles Philip Arthur George.

The people outside cheered because they knew this tiny boy probably would grow up to be king of England. Now he rested in a cradle. It had been used by his mother when she was a baby.

Princess Elizabeth was 22 years old when Charles was born. She was the older daughter of King George VI. She had one sister, but no brothers.

Princess Elizabeth and Prince Philip loved their baby son. Prince Philip was in the Royal Navy. He had to be away from home part of the time. And Princess Elizabeth had work to do for her country.

A nanny or nursemaid took good care of the tiny prince. Whenever his mother could get time, she played with him in the nursery and gave him his evening bath.

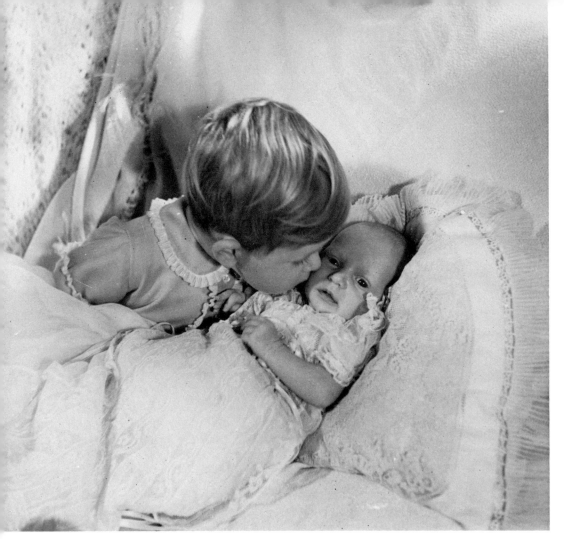

Prince Charles and his sister. Princess Anne.

Before Charles was two years old, a baby sister was born. She was called Princess Anne.

Charles loved his baby sister. When she grew bigger, they played together.

Charles liked to visit his grandfather, King George, and his grandmother, the Queen. He liked to help his grandmother work in her garden. One day he decided to work in the garden by himself. With his little shovel, he dug up a whole row of tulip bulbs that had just been planted. The Queen didn't think Prince Charles was helpful that day!

When Charles was three years old, his grandfather, the King, died. Everyone was sad.

The family moved into Buckingham Palace, where Charles had been born. His mother took her father's place. She was now the Queen.

A special ceremony was held at Westminster Abbey. The Queen rode there in a golden coach. Charles went later. He was just in time to see the crown put on her head.

Preparing to place the crown on the head of the Queen.

Buckingham Palace has 600 rooms and many hall-ways. There are many places for a young prince to play.

In the Grand Hall, Charles drove his little car around and parked it behind one of the marble stat-ues.

LONGLAC PUBLIC LIBRARY

Or he played with his wooden horse and carriage.

Sometimes, he played with his sister, Anne. Charles and Anne liked to play dress-up games. He pretended he was king. He put on a red cape and carried a toy sword. Anne pretended she was queen. Other times they dressed as cowboys and Indians.

11

Some afternoons, the Queen had time to play with the children in the garden.

Charles liked to play with his rabbit, Harvey. Charles had a dog named Whiskey, and Anne had a dog named Sherry. Charles also had a pet hamster.

Charles loved parades and marching bands. He tooted his toy trumpet and marched through the palace halls. He liked to watch the band play for the people outside the palace.

One day, people were surprised to see the little prince pretending to conduct the band from a palace window.

Charles was usually a good boy, and very polite. But he sometimes got into mischief. One day, he made a face at a crowd. His dad gave him a spanking. Prince Philip wanted Charles to remember that he must be polite to the people. Someday, he would be their king.

When Charles was five years old, he could write his name. His mother had taught him to count and to read some words.

Now the Queen hired a teacher for him. Every morning he had school in the palace nursery.

Later, Charles went to a special school near the palace with about 100 boys.

Charles and Anne reading in the picture Gallery at Buckingham Palace.

Charles needed to get to know London, the city where he lived. But everywhere he went, people stopped to stare at him. The Queen didn't want Charles to feel he was special. She wanted him to be like other boys. So he and his nursemaid used to ride around the city in a very old Ford. No one guessed that inside that old car was the prince.

Charles visited the railroad underground, and even bought his own ticket for a train ride. He visited many places in London, and no one guessed who he was.

One year, Charles visited a store to talk to Father Christmas. He told Father Christmas that he wanted a bicycle.

At Christmas, the family went to another home they owned, called Sandringham. It was a long way from London, so they took a train.

Charles and Anne, with a little help from some grown-ups, made a big snowman in front of the house.

Charles liked to draw and paint. Each year, he made Christmas cards for his family.

One year, Charles got a drum for Christmas. But some of the grown-ups took turns playing with it before he had a turn.

LONGLAC PUBLIC LIBRARY

He also got an electric train. His dad showed him how to operate it. His dad kept moving cars and running the train through tunnels. Charles had to go to bed before he had a chance to play with the train.

Very early the next morning, a servant found Charles in the hall.

"Where are you going?" the servant asked.

"I'm going to play with my train, if it isn't broken already," said the prince.

Charles liked to find out about things. Everywhere he went, he asked questions. He even asked the cook questions. Sometimes the cook let him help make cookies and do other things.

One day, Charles and Anne went to the storehouse to get some eggs for the cook. On the way upstairs, Charles dropped the pan of eggs. Can you guess what happened?

When Charles was eight years old, he went to a school called Cheam.

Charles lived at the school. He slept in a large room with nine other boys. Each morning, he had to make his bed. He had to fold or hang his clothes and polish his shoes. No one treated him like a prince.

All the boys dressed alike. Each wore a gray jacket.

There were three classes after breakfast each morning. Then the boys had a mug of milk and a bun. There were two more classes before lunch, at one o'clock.

Prince Charles and some of his classmates at Cheam.

In the afternoon, the boys had sports and crafts. Charles liked to make things. One year, he made a wooden book rack for his mother and a small table for his sister.

The Royal Family at Balmoral.

Charles went home for Christmas and for summer vacations. In the summer, the family went to Balmoral. That is another home they own. By now, there were three children, Charles, Anne, and Andrew. Later, a fourth child would be born, named Edward.

At Balmoral, the family often had picnics or went to the beach. Charles and his father caught fish, and Prince Philip cooked them on his grill.

Prince Philip and the two older children liked to camp out near the shore of Loch Muick. They slept in sleeping bags and sometimes caught fish for breakfast.

When Charles was 14, he went to a school in Scotland. Nearly 400 boys lived at Gordonstoun. Here Charles had to help empty wastebaskets and sweep the floors every day. He took his turn raking the gravel path and working in the flower beds.

Prince Charles takes
part in a school play.

At this school, Charles was very busy. He didn't
have much time to do what he wanted. There were
even classes on Saturday mornings.

Charles sang in the school choir and played the
trumpet in the school orchestra. He also had parts in
some school plays. He won an award in a lifesaving
class. His parents were proud of him.

Charles went to school in Australia for a year. Timbertop is in wild, rough country, far from a city. Charles worked hard at this school too. And when he went home, everyone noticed how tall he had grown. Prince Charles was growing up.

Charles went back to Gordonstoun and was chosen to be the head boy of the house where he lived.

Prince Charles in Australia.

Prince Charles and his brother, Prince Andrew, aboard a ship.

Later, Prince Charles went to Cambridge College for two years. He was also in the Royal Navy, like his father. He likes boats—big ones and little ones.

He learned to pilot a plane and to do many other things young men like to do.

In Canada, Prince Charles helps celebrate the 100th Anniversary of the signing of a peace treaty.

Now that he is a man, Prince Charles works for his country. He visits many countries. He makes speeches. He talks with many people.

Everywhere he goes, people like Prince Charles. He is kind, polite, and enjoys a good joke.

LONGLAC PUBLIC LIBRARY

All his life, Prince Charles has been learning how
to do things.

One thing he is learning about still is how to be a
good king. Someday, he will take his mother's place.
He will sit on the throne. He will be King of England
and its territories.

We wish to thank the following agencies for permission
to use their photos.
Associated Press, page 28.
Black Star, page 10.
Camera Press, pages 6 and 15.
Keystone, pages 4, 23, and 25.
United Press International, pages 9, 11, 29, and 30.